In the Presence of Love

Raw Emotion Series

Book One

By

Ernesto Ortiz

authorHOUSE™

1663 LIBERTY DRIVE, SUITE 200
BLOOMINGTON, INDIANA 47403
(800) 839-8640
WWW.AUTHORHOUSE.COM

© 2006 Ernesto Ortiz. All rights reserved.

No part of this book may be reproduced, stored in a retrieval system, or transmitted by any means without the written permission of the author.

First published by AuthorHouse 9/26/2006

ISBN: 1-4259-9994-8 (e)
ISBN: 1-4259-9993-X (sc)

Library of Congress Control Number: 2005907345
Printed in the United States of America
Bloomington, Indiana

This book is printed on acid-free paper.

Dedication

There is a unique experience that many of us have at one time in our lives or another, that is the experience of falling in love, falling in love not only with another human but deeply and passionately falling in love with God the Divine. This has happened to me to the point of having my heart burning, consumed by that love; I have recognized that this is a very personal feeling one that can not be described so what I have done is write the felling as they come to me.

This book is dedicated to you the reader, the seeker, to my children and more specially the Beloved. With the hope that it will give you some inspiration and awaken that inner desire for God/Goddess... All there is.

Ernesto

I've realized that is more important to look at the wind and the clouds than to worry about the past.
That I much rather give to someone I love than to take them for granted.
That it's Ok to do nothing sometimes.
That it's Ok to appear crazy in the eyes of others as I enjoy life.
That it's Ok to do childish, playful silly things in public even though I am 45
That it's Ok to dance and feel the freedom of going wild.
That it's Ok to be silent and make a connection with the Divine.
That it's Ok to say I LOVE YOU when you feel it in your heart.
That it's Ok to call your friends and spend some quality time.
That It's Ok to use my good clothing every day and not just let it hang.
To make every day a special occasion and celebrate from the heart.

*Not to wait till Christmas to give a gift,
but to make it a surprise.
To order the best thing from the menu
instead of saving $5.95
To make someone that I meet a clerk,
a waiter, feel special by giving them an
honest smile.
To cherish special moments with my lover
as if this was our last.
To flavor life to it's fullest every day,
every hour, every minute, every sunrise
and sunset. To celebrate every breath I
take as a magnificent gift from God.*

Today I beheld the lovely face of the Beloved. I looked into her eyes glowing like two bright lanterns the more I looked the more I melted a puddle of hot melted wax. The heart spoke; I will yield to the feelings of the soul. The soul joined in bringing the music from on high a concert a melody inspired by this light. The soul sang; in love all things are transformed. The body joined and danced the dance of ecstasy and passion. The lovely face looked at the body and joined in the dance of two souls dancing the sacred dance of love, marriage and passion.

Love is the ultimate essence of life
what we look for, what we seek, what
we fear when we find it. This love
can be the union the connection with
God/Goddess with the inner child this
love can help us (me) to grow wings
to fly. From on high I can see observe
and allow life. Surrender to this love
my friend if you think you have found
it, ask for help from the Divine and be
ready to enjoy the ride.

I have seen you, I have felt you after this experience how can I ever forget you. I have taken you in so deep within that I don't think I need my eyes or my hands any more. I don't want to see or feel any other than you my love.

I would love to kiss you my princess and hold you in my arms. Hold you so tight that we become one and in that ecstasy melt with the Divine till we feel no difference men, woman, God, Goddess, earth and sky.

Fine water molecules that dance above the waters surface weightless and free. The water responds and ripples all over, deep beneath. The water molecules move as they come up to the surface to unite in a cosmic dance, the water is dancing throughout.

My soul is in love, passionately madly in love with you my Beloved.

I am so hungry for you that I feel that I can devour you. The more I have you, the more I want you. This is Divine hunger translated to the expression of human feelings and sensations.
What appetite I have for you today.
Be ready for me.

Enter this place my sweet lover it has been prepared for you. It may feel a bit strange to you, the newness of it all but trust that it is for you. Come my love and enter the secret chamber and see what awaits for you there. This is your place within me, the place you can call home. This place as you can see has many rooms. Where we can be together and can be free. There is plenty of room to expand your wings without the constriction of the old me.

Time has been taken to create this new place and all I can tell you, is that the greatest builder of all times has come to help me, and He has designed this place for you and me.

In order to make love grow we have to tend to it like a precious garden. Every day nurture it, weed it, and fertilize it. Do it for the sake of love alone and not for the magnificent harvest.

If I could I would take some stars and string them as a necklace for you.
If I could I would take some planets and create a staircase to Heaven for you.
If I could I would take a million flower petals and create a carpet for you to walk on.
If I could I would take some dewdrops and color them to create a picture for you.
If I could I would compose a love song and give it to the angels to sing.
If I could I would roll around in the clouds with you.
If I could I would win the lottery for you.
If I could I would bottle God's healing energy and give it to you.
If I could I would create an international commercial to tell the world that I love you.
If I could I would kiss you from head to toe everyday from morning till night.
If I could I would dive the ocean to find the most precious pearls to make earrings to match the stars.

If I could I would give you the jewels from the crown of England.
But what I can do is give you the pearls and jewels of my inspiration.
I can give you sunsets filled with passion and love.
I can give you my tenderness and support.
I can give you the dream of a life fulfilled and the vision of us as an old couple walking down the beach.
I can give you romantic moments filled with tender touches and kisses.
I can give you every day an open heart full of love.
I can give you the promise of eternal love.

I think of you and my body shivers it sends a tingle up and down my spine. What magic do you posses that with a simple thought this can happen to me? Electrical currents that have intensified the more I know you the more I grow. The more I grow the more I like what I see about you and me.

Self, open your heart to love. To the pleasures of life that must be shared Love and passion. Touch sensual sexual feelings that can open the senses and emotions to other dimensions and possibilities of life and ecstasy. Self drop your guard down and allow it to be.

There is a beautiful rainbow in the sky hiding behind the clouds. Look up my love and see if you can find it because it is holding a message of love and harmony from my heart.

Touch me with the passion that you would have if this was the only opportunity for us being together. Touch me as if this was the last day of my life. Touch me everyday as if this was our last day together.

I am devouring life as if this day was my last meal. I rather devour you. I am thinking of the night, the smells and sounds and they fill me.
Magnetic changes take place within me; I feel the expansion like floating in the middle of the Milky Way. Floating, floating away in this endless sea of love. I float towards you. Love so sweet and deep float away with me.

In the month of May when the days grow long the trees go to flower and welcome the birds, the air changes and so do I. Parted from love opened my heart to the deepest love I am able to share.

You in my life goddess, spirit, heart. Opening and blossoming before my eyes, in the month of May, celebration of life.

I have loved but never like this before. My joy is present when I ask to share a life that is what happened in the month of May.

Heart oh heart; you hold within you all the mystery of my life. You surprise me and have kept me in love with the splendor and the beauty of a feeling that can only be compared to being in love.

If energy can intoxicate, then I am drunk my love. If sounds create music, I am dancing my love. If wind moves then I am flying my love.

Your light touches me your love is what makes me write. You move my heart as if it where a pen to express this poetry that comes from the heart.

I admire the romance, the dance of the shadows with the light. Sensually moving in and out of each other like two lovers in the dark.

Sometimes a little stimulation can provide the juices of creation, the excitement of a new adventure of pleasure and delight.

I look at the Beloved with hungry eyes, with desire and passion. Let me seduce you in the most intimate way, let me get consumed with you, disappear into your essence, get drunk with your mystery. Embrace me with your arms of love.

Falling asleep last night I looked into the eyes of the Beloved. I made a vow to get deeper into you. If I smell a rose without your love, it would be a wasted fragrance.

A vow, a promise to find the precious garden within us, sprinkle it with love and get intoxicated in the fragrance.

I think about you so much my sweet Beloved, wanting you, desiring you, stretching my arms to hold you and to feel the tenderness of your heart. Let me hear the whisper of your voice so close to my ear that I can take you in. Let me hold you in my arms so you can feel me. Give me what you can while I give you what I have. Wrap me in your mantle of a million stars, set me free to fly and jump from star to star.

I imagine the skin of my lover soft, wet, soapy, and me indulging on the energy created by two hearts by two lovers that allow the elements to caress their bodies.

Passion arises from my heart and I allow my hands, my body to explore to explore yours in this liquid element. The thirst that we feel gets satisfied by the time that we spend together in this liquid passion of delight.

I can't take you out of my mind you are ever present at every moment you are there. I miss you like the flowers miss the rain, like a thirsty man a glass of water, I miss you.
I close my eyes and see your smile, I feel the warm air and imagine is your skin. At night I feel the sheets and I imagine you there, your scent is present and I.... Can not go to sleep, I am day dreaming in the middle of the night. One thing I know, I love you and I miss you my love.

I think of you and I get goose bumps all over. I think of your silky skin and I want to touch it with the tenderness and passion that I would use to touch a precious fabric that has been woven with the finest of threads. But not even that can possibly compare to the sensations that I get when I caress your body with the tenderness and passion of a men, a lover a twin flame.

*She came and touched me once again
I felt the magic and the beauty once
again. Why is it that what I am
feeling has to come to an end? From
one dolphin to another here I am your
departing lover and friend. The ocean
is deep but I know it well. We'll swim
separate till we unite again. Water
is our element as we float in a sea of
emotions. I will never forget you my
lover and twin flame.*

This golden sunlight is bathing my body charging it with light. And my thoughts go and wonder to you, my afternoon delight. Images of the shadows that follow your shape in this golden sunlight as my hands caress your body, as if they were the wind, warm soft, sensual, full of the qualities of a loving heart.

The nectar of spring is so close to
my lips I can almost taste it. The
sweetness, the fragrance of your lips
are like an intoxicating wine one
that is saved and flavored on special
occasions. But why has to be only
in spring, why it has to be a special
occasion when I want to be intoxicated
all the time.

Nothing in the world compares to the feelings of an open heart!

I feel this love that is burning like a fire out of control. Kisses without lips passion without a body to share it with, how do I put this fire out Lord? How do I transform the feelings of passion into love?

Times come and go, time to learn and take in, time to enjoy and share and time to love and live in love. Times come and go, I am glad to know that my time to love is here and here to stay.

I am experiencing the ecstasy of the Divine feminine genderless sensations run through my body and she, the Divine Mother clothed with the glow of a million stars stares at me. Take me in become me, balance, intuition. The jade gate opens to welcome the masculine principle and the I, stands alone observing watching it all unfold.

Your body is like a fine instrument. I pluck your stings and you vibrate creating the finest and most beautiful music. It is sensual and undulating. I caress you with the tenderness that one would have with something precious. Your music enters my body and creates feelings and sensations that mix with your own to celebrate the music of our hearts and souls.

My heart is full of passion and desire, hungry to devour you my Beloved. Open to feel the closeness of your breath, the sweet whisper of your voice in my ear and the warmth of your embrace all over my body. Take me to new heights, take me up to the light, invite me to your home, your bed and cuddle me at night, till my breath seizes to exist and becomes part of the One.

Love is a spiritual experience. The question is how do we get there? First love thyself; be thyself; know thyself and love will come as a reward from beyond.

I want to celebrate life with you, and the freedom of individuality in love. I want to get lost in the ecstasy of our love, surrender into the unknown and trust that I can discover with you love and life, the sacred.

I want to learn how to fulfill your fantasies so you can get lost in the arms of love.

I cannot hold back what I have to give you. What I am, what I have, and what I am becoming.

It is because of your love that I am here, this inspiration, this passion for life is because of you my Beloved. How can I ever repay you for bringing me back to life?

I will keep thee in my heart because is there where you belong!

My experience with love has been unique and rewarding like climbing a mountain, many times I felt that I've reach the peak just to find that I was not near the end.

I've had had bruises, and cuts, broken bones, exhaustion, anger, of course a broken heart.

The rewards have been many as well, the feelings of joy, and expansion, pleasure and ecstasy, intimacy and sex all nice, but more than anything the ability and capacity to love.

*Love how can I find myself going into
other arms after I have felt you?
Stay with me and continue giving me
comfort and joy, give me the essence of
who you are no more no less but give
it all to me, because after you I don't
want to experience other love, my love,
my beloved.*

My mind has the freedom of a bird that has been let out of a cage. My heart trembles when my gaze rests in you. My soul sings when in your presence, and I take in the sunlight from your touch.

I asked and she said yes! A kaleidoscope of colors appeared in our lives. Changed infused with love and passion, multi colored images that unite with splendor. The gate of the future appears and it's open. Enter in and dance.

*I dive into the splendor of your care,
I enter sliding slowly, observing,
feeling this sacred temple of the Divine
feminine, an experience, an adventure
as I feel the soft and silky walls of
your space. I dive in deep I feel the
hot and steamy air sliding fast in
the decent and slowing down on the
ascent. The explorer is using his tools
and intuition he knows how special
this is, the cave rumbles creating
sounds that come from deep inside,
like a volcano ready to erupt. I and the
cave become one as we melt with the
lava of ecstasy, flowing unobstructed
burning through till the volcano is
empty satisfied and resting in a place
called the heart.*

Warm milk and honey happy moments and sensations that come close to the brushing of the wings of angels over my body and yours my Beloved. Playful melodies warm whispers and the caress, the touch of love all over my body.
Kundalini the magic serpent is rising, rising expanding within me and you, as the full participant of the experience with me. Warm milk and honey how sweet it is.

I am drinking liquid Light. Oh what a feeling, of sensual delight. My senses have awakened to this pleasure from on high.
Give me more, as my cup is empty of this precious Light.

Love, did you see the fool moon in the sky? I've been having a conversation with her. I told her about my feelings, I opened my heart she smiled at me and with a brilliant face whispered in my ear it was loud and clear. She said; Brother Sun I am your sister moon the only thing you have to do is follow your heart and give it some action, manifest your destiny and your dreams. I've seen it done before and you my dear brother know it too.

Happiness is not fully achieved unless it is shared and Love cannot expand unless it is freely given.

Morning afternoon and evening I think of you. The thoughts consume me. I feel drenched like the earth must feel after a heavy rain, saturated and full, preparing the soul to give birth to new ideas, things, places to go and more feelings to cultivate and have. Do you think of me as much as I think of you? I'll never know. But are you ready to get drenched, to prepare your soul? I am, and for that I love to be consumed by the thoughts of you.

The night has fallen and you are not there, it is time to go to bed. How I miss your presence, there is emptiness a void. Nothing I can do tonight if you are not here. My heart is full but my bed is empty, I guess I can go to my heart to fill in the emptiness in my bed.

Your face is the light that makes my body tingle; your eyes are the windows to your soul. Deep inside I see the moon and the stars. The whole universe as it appears reflected in your eyes. For a moment time is suspended into eternity as I enter in your eyes.

I wonder if you dream of me as much as I dream of you, if your days are filled with warm thoughts and exciting visions as are mine.

You my Beloved cut me loose to go on my own journey, as you embark on your own. Like two trees that where entwined, and now no more, side by side but separate, growing on our own. The leaves shimmer in the sunshine and in the morning they hold the dewdrops. Seasons come and go the sun and the moon keeps looking down at us. But only you my Beloved know what is beneath the earth as the roots grow.

Today I am dreaming of an old reality of tongue, lips and tangled bodies as we made love. Passion come to me and just for today let's get together in sweet harmony of love making and tangled tongues, lips and more.

*A lover longs to love he has no choice.
A lover longs to kiss your soft lips he has no choice.
A lover longs to play with the locks in your hair he has no choice.
A lover longs to touch your skin, your body, to make passionate love he has no choice.
A lover longs to feel ecstasy in the union of two tangled bodies he has no choice. A lover longs to let go of limitations and fears he has no choice.
A lover longs to be humble in the presence of love he has no choice.
A lover longs for self- love he has no choice.
A lover longs to love you.*

In my quiet moments I think of you.
In my busy time, you are present in my mind.
When I dream… I dream of you.
You are so present in my mind and occupying the seat of honor in my heart.

I want to know that I can be spontaneous with my love, and that it will be well received. I want to know that I can be demonstrative with my actions that I can be crazy and free and that it will not be judge. I want to show what I feel inside without anything to hide and that it will be all right for me.

Let me indulge in the feast of life, like a lavish orgy that can feed my senses. Let me devour nature and partake in the sensual feeding of life. Let me pretend that as I surrender to this feast I am devouring you, my Beloved. Let the internal feelings of this feast be reflected in my outer reality. Let me devour you till I can't make the distinction from the dream and the reality. Show me how to partake in this lavish feast with you my love.

I wonder what you looked like this morning when you first open your eyes. Did you have a smile in your face and stretched your arms as you greeted the day?
I wonder if you heard the sounds of birds signing outside and if that made you feel full and alive?
I wonder how your spirit fills this morning. Is it vibrant and alive?
I wonder what was your first thought this morning as you laid naked in bed, did the thought of me crosses your mind. If it did, I wonder if it made your heart sing.
I wonder if when you moved to make your cup of coffee, you felt in the air the presence, the scent of me.
I wonder how your heart feels today.
I wish I could have seen your face…..

Forty nine kisses and a glass of wine, the intention on which are given can make me dance, feel like I am floating on cloud 49. Airy feet that hardly move but keep the rhythm of this song, this melody that makes me feel that the music comes from the inside.

Thinking of my Beloved sends a wave of quivers down my spine I long to feel the touch and rhythm of her undulating mind.

Is this caress the hand of God, the Beloved or is it the embodiment of the feminine Divine, as this all appears in my mind.

Makes no difference because as I perceive it, is all one.

Be patient with me while I look at your face, let me sit by your side and daydream.

Without you and my dream my life is empty and the road long and hard. My eyes engage and sing a new song I can see the reflection of you in me.

Love stay and sing this new song with me, and let's fall into the silence of the dream.

If you fill your heart with love, if you fill every atom of your essence with love, when anger enters it will be instantly dissolved.
Why? Because anger cannot live in love.

The sweet nectar of life flows before me everyday like a river with undulating curves caressing the silky warm waters bathing me in purple cellophane that wraps me like a cocoon. The warm touch, caress of your hand adds to my experience I feel bathed by your sweet nectar. Love shows up at my door every day, how do I treat you? Like a stranger that is not welcome or as a long lost friend? Give me pleasure and satisfaction life, I am your friend, your lover and you are my mate.

*I sit quietly looking, wanting and
wishing to know what to do.
What can I do when I know it is out
of my hands?
Love is the only thing that I can do,
love that transcends the physical
condition, love that is pure and simple
given and received unconditionally,
love that is free just like the best things
in life, air, sunshine, the stars at night.
Love that fills the heart.*

Drenched in a sea of emotions hearts pounding as we embrace as one, excitement in shallow waters as clear and blue as the sky. Two bodies melting into their elements water, air sunshine, alive with emotion two bodies melting as one.

If I could only express what is deep in my heart my love, feelings, sensations, emotions of love that cannot be explained but can be shared.
Only once in my life I have felt this way, only once in my life I have loved from the depths of my soul as I love you my love, lover, Beloved.

Walking down the Silk Road the desert of life, the splendor of the day jumps at me and clings like the sky to the sun. Reflections and dreams are the oasis of life; the mystery unfolds before my eyes. A lone date tree bares his sweet fruit in abundance, juicy and delicious is the nectar of life, abundant like the sand of the desert and hot like the fire of the heart.

I drink wine and get intoxicated, light headed and I think of you… I love to kiss you and taste the sweetness of your lips. Kissing you has the same effect as drinking wine, but without the side effects.

I do not express in speech and with elegance, I have your love in my heart. If I walk through a field of flowers without your guidance and your love, if I stop to smell a rose the fragrance would burn my nose. If I get in bed without you, I will experience a love less night. If I run against the wind and I don't feel you, I should wonder if I am dead or alive. I am like a seed waiting for spring waiting to grow; I am like a sunflower looking up, looking up to you to get the warmth of the sun.

The fantasy of love is like a butterfly flying aimlessly from flower to flower touching the nectar of inspiration provided by the sweetness of the moment we call love.

Then there is rest in the arms of the Beloved and the reassurance that love Divine is possible it is inspired only by the love for the self with the understanding that selfish love is the only kind of love that can be shared from the bottom of the heart.

A soft caress a touch, a tender look from the Beloved, electric currents bolts of blue lightning that enter and explode within me. Longing to rest in her arms to melt into the essence of the Divine feminine to re-charge covered by the mantle of 1000 stars.

*My love for you keeps lifting me
higher. This I have never experienced
before. Life doesn't seem to be the same
any more. There is a certain quality
a vibration an aliveness of all things.
The sky is open and beautiful even
through darkened clouds.
I feel the connection with myself
growing richer, deeper and stronger,
and that I know I can share with you.*

The full expression of Divine Love is taking over my body. It comes in to re adjust and heal. I feel renewed in the presence of the Beloved. I surrender to Love.

Pay close attention and listen my heart to the soft whispering of service. Feelings from the reward is how I make love to you.

Anyone that resides in the power of love is free to have an open heart. To be touched with his/hers inner power, to be connected and never separated, always free and giving and always open to continued growth.

*I have longed to touch you, to kiss you,
to taste the sweetness of your lips. The
price for this is your life.
What a bargain lets run and buy it,
and buy it now.*

Out of union come God, Goddess, and male, female duality sacred manifestations of the Divine, power, wisdom, love. That can make some hearts tremble others feel right at home. Seeking, searching to achieve the balance the mix, like water for chocolate and when is done a little sprinkle of sweetness for the final touch.

*When I die, don't be disturbed my love
if you come close to me to kiss me good
bye and I open my eyes to see.*

The thirsty lover comes to the Beloved full of love and desire. Looking deeply into quenching his thirst, I taste your sweet essence and quench my thirst. I find no words to describe the love that I am tasting the kind of love that is capable of sending me into a world of ecstasy and paradise.

The sound of two flutes is echoing in the canyon the notes move like two lovers when making love, slow and seductive then fast and furious keeping the balance and the harmony in love. The walls of the mountains respond to the energy and vibrate with color and sound an aliveness is felt that is creating a web.

And now that the flutes have stopped playing the strings from the web will keep on vibrating the sound of the two flutes for eternity.

Thinking of you makes me feel drunk, my head spins and my senses get altered. Hypersensitive with only an image to dream about, wishing to pull you closer and feel this intoxication in my physical reality and not just in daydream.

The magic that is possible during our union makes me want to explore the sensual pleasures that can be achieved by being willing to explore and discover how to have a multitude of sacred orgasms that can only lead to new heights. The awareness of what it means to be in love with a full connection of our being and one heart.

Tonight she looked beautiful she took my breath away. Her skin soft and pearly white, eyes that looked right through me. She knew what I was thinking, feeling. I was caressing her with my eyes; her undulating body moved she danced. I watched her movements. The more she moved the more I became drunk, intoxicated with feelings and emotions that made me feel alive.

I feel like I am falling, falling, falling in love with you again. What a beautiful feeling to be suspended in the ecstasy of love again.

My soul has been searching, learning by trial and error, looking for the Beloved. Knowing that total fusion is possible; maturity is essential, understanding and an open heart. Fusion that leads to an explosion of all senses to sacred union ecstasy and bliss,
I think about it, I feel it and there it is present like a tingle or millions of butterflies flapping their wings within me. Your image comes and I go to that space that we have shared, the place of fusion, love and bliss.

My connection is intact my love is so pure that all I want to do is give it to you. Open up my love to feel and let it enter deep within. If I don't express it, if I don't give it, it will go to waist. Thank God I have you and the Beloved to pour it in.

I choose to live in love. What a glorious gift to feel that I can choose the feelings that enter my heart, like food for the soul. Today my choice is peace and serenity and the expansion of what I have been nurturing in my heart.

I painted her face copper and gold. She painted mine; we became a mirror of each other, glistening, sparkling deepening into a space of expressive art. Two sculptures are becoming alive, experiencing transformation as a woman and a man, experiencing union, connecting heart to heart, becoming and expanding each other's hearts.

*Oh, from your sweet mouth I have
come to know passion and love, from
you I have been able to be transported
to realms not known before. From your
sweet caress I have learned how to
return a touch that goes beneath the
skin, from your eyes I have been able
to see and appreciate the blue likeness
of the sky and the depth of an ocean
filled with mysteries and treasures,
from what makes you be I have learned
to love, love so deep like I have never
experienced before.
What we have shared together,
deep passion and love is the link we
acknowledge to tie our souls.
You my Beloved will be present in my
life for eternity and more.*

Listen my heart to the whispering of my soul it's telling you this is how I make love to you.

I have sent you many letters that I write in the face of the moon. Look up my love and you will find them there. Wait till the full moon and she will sprinkle moon dust on you filled with the essence of my love for you.

Precious moments of ecstasy and love, minutes that I want to turn into hours. Kisses shared, sweet as honey. Nothing compares to this sweetness, honey that runs down your body and I want to taste it, passion that engulfs me. I feel consumed in this dream state. Reality comes back to me, but not right now let me stay in this dream for a while. I want this passion to run through my veins like the blood that feeds me and nourishes my body, passion that I dream of passion that I want to feel and share with you my eternal love.

The ecstasy of love is like a single golden grain of sand on the beach. Lucky are the ones that find it.

My heart is open she said… I am experiencing so much passion that I want to be consumed in an embrace of love. My heart gets melted into this pool of feelings and desire to experience this passion this love in a way that I have never experienced before.

I woke up with an open heart remembering sweet dreams and the longing to be with you again. I want that connection Lord.

The desire grows like the desire of a lover for his sweet loving mate, the desire for your touch and your embrace. Get close to me sweet lover let me feel your face. Your breath close to my ear will make me feel safe.

A symphony is ringing in my ears, the
colors and the sounds suddenly appear.
Sweet harmonies like cotton candy
weaving in and out my ears.
Are these the sounds of love, the
sounds that wake the heart to dance?
YES, this is what I feel; the fullness of
life is inside my ears.
Sweet harmony of life, stay ringing in
my ears.

The sound of your voice is like particles of love that enter my ear to disperse in my body to bring harmony and remove all fear. The soothing of my heart like the gentle caress of a waterfall as it splashes on my body washing away bringing harmony, love and consuming all fear.

*If you have lost the path towards love,
turn to me and let me guide you back
to the heart.*

Sweet mystery you come into my life and surprise me. You open my heart, my passion, my imagination, and then you hide from me, leaving me confused and empty.

You peek out to show me you are there, but I can't have you. Sweet mystery my heart is longing for you and for the fullness of the expression of love.

Look at me because I shall become your companion look at me straight in the eyes, find yourself deep inside me and open to begin an adventure that has all the potential to last. Hear my voice calling like the howl of the wolf or the cry the whale.

Mountains and oceans merge with one another to become one like heaven and earth. Feel my passion, my heart as I share it don't keep yourself veiled to my eyes. I rejoice in the splendor of your beauty in the brilliance of your smile. Love is intoxicating it makes me dizzy like wine, the soft glow of the candle the fragrance of the incense all contribute to my feelings the vision of the union the path, the companion. Keep your gaze on me and look deep into my eyes.

Yesterday I was down and now I am up I was hurt and now I am healed, I was weeping and now I am laughing. The power of love came over me and now I feel Grace and everlasting love. My eyes where blurry and now I can see, I have the heart of a lion, the body of the gazelle and the powerful spirit of the monkey. I am not intoxicated I am alive as I can be, or maybe I am intoxicated with joy.

This silence is so loud that I can hardly hear you. I must move to the roar of the waterfall to hear you. The inner silence that I know will take me close to you.

His flute echoes the melodies from his heart soft and inspiring that sometimes make you cry and other times you tap your feet and all you can do is dance. Flute payer, play your flute and let your heart be the music of inspiration that makes me love to dance and cry.

My flute is playing for you whether you hear it or not, the sound of love is coming in. When the flute hits the highest note I reach out and stretch for you, for your love and your tenderness. The flute plays on the melody of love penetrating this body, piercing through walls, the notes are millions of feelings as sun beams of light. Where have you heard music sound like this?

The grapes get crushed slowly and delicately, the juice ferments as the new wine squeezed from desire. The ingredients of this new body wine milk and honey. The bodies of the lovers bake the bread mmmmmmm….. Let's drink the wine and have a banquet with the rest.

I am embracing life with the passion of this moment. Devouring every second with my eyes, allowing life to consume me as I consume life.
Life becomes a banquet of passion and delight, how can I say anything other than yes, to what the Beloved is serving me? So I say yes, to life.

Love for you Lord makes me be so obvious to others. Your love has rooted out of my feet to structure my wellbeing. Love only desires to be love, love accepts and gives freely of itself and looks for an open heart to share. Love is intensity and magic, the magic of renunciation and acceptance. Love is patient and open, kind and forgiving, love's fire is passionate and creative, love surfaces at a glance at the wink of an eye and the flapping of the wings of a butterfly.

Like an angel she descended planting one foot at a time on the steps of my reality. Translucent and transparent are her wings caressing me softly, allowing me to feel her skin, the energy of an angel like no other. Sensuous undulating body, inviting smile, lips dripping with sweet raspberry juice, oh so kissable.

I asked for her name May Lee she whispered softly in my ear. Her breath entered my body like the fine mist that can only come from heaven. May Lee stay with me for a minute an hour a year or a lifetime? Lets shape shift together spread our wings and fly, touching people not with two but with four hands. Let them receive the energy of an angel and two loving hearts.

Thinking of the beloved and wanting to dance. I wonder if she is willing to dance in the moonlight, to dance barefoot in the dirt. To eat a feast with our hands and let the juice drip down our arms? To let go a balloon with a wish and a prayer to climb a tree, to look foolish in the eyes of others while dancing in the streets, celebrating life, love and passion. I wonder if she dreams with me.

The chemistry of love is like walking in the rain without an umbrella, it is inevitable that you'll get wet. The question is, are you going to run and hide from it? Or become child like care free and enjoy getting wet.

Now what? I am soaking wet and so is the beloved, the natural garments are translucent showing every curve of her delicious body I drink the rain and get lost in the thunderstorm of emotions. The water flows caressing our bodies, piercing eyes. All of this happening in a fragment of time, the chemistry of love or is it the chemistry of lust?

She dances like a goddess moving like the wind soft, sensual warm, caressing my body with the energy of the movement of her hands, touching my soul. I feel the wind not the flesh, fine silk with sparks of gold in the night, flowing as she moves illuminating the movements of her dance. Touch me with your garment and embrace me with your soul move within me as you move with the wind.

What to do when we encounter the newness of an open heart... Push, push against the natural resistance, the forces of humanity that say, close it, protect it, is not safe.

But this is not what I want... Is it a risk to keep it open? Push, push against the resistance, only if you do that you will discover the beauty of what lies behind, the hidden treasures that come from the courage of having an open heart.

Sweet Mystery of life I'm glad I found you. At times I have felt like a child playing hide and go seek. Looking, looking and not finding you but knowing you where there. Sensing feeling that I was getting close to catch a glimpse of you, like a shadow that escapes into the next corner, eluding me. When all I wanted to do is catch you and hold you in a long embrace.

My heart is so full that is dripping with emotion. Picture this, a honey filled heart that is dripping all over, slow, sweet, giving, offering this succulent juice to my love my lover the Beloved. Taste it and get intoxicated with me as I allow the sweetness to flow through me.

I am filling my heart with the Spirit of God. What a beautiful feeling is entering my heart. Is like a shoot of electricity that comes down my body. It is vibrating alive. What a moment of ecstasy is entering my heart. I am exploding with it. Let me share it with you as you pass by.

*The first time I looked into your eyes
I remembered. Then I started looking.
Then I found you and lost you. Finally
I surrendered just to find out that in
doing that I discovered!*

Music you enter my body and make me dance, you caress me from the inside out. You take me to new levels of feelings and sensations you bring me to connect with my body as a vehicle of expression of the Sacred and the Divine.

Have I told you lately what you mean to me? That your energy is indispensable in my life, that I like fresh flowers will wither without your love. You the Beloved give me a reason for being a reason to love and serve.

Your energy is magnetic and beautiful. You sit in the Light of God and I am able to be a witness and partake of the Light you are so close to, the light of the Beloved. You are the Beloved.

Morning, afternoon and evening I think of the Beloved and welcome her in my heart. What a beautiful recognition that this is the food that fuels my life.
I was a thirsty and hungry man until I fully recognized that life is not life without love, the kind of love that appreciates and honors that food that fuels the heart.

Being consumed by the ecstasy of life, being willing to be who I am. Does the rose pretend to be something that she is not? Let me continue learning from nature to be real, and to simply pretend to be who I am.

I want to experience life as if this was my last day here, giving myself to fully living. Living with an open heart, claiming daily what I choose to have present in my life, and refusing the things and feelings that will prevent me from experiencing this life in love, beauty, harmony, peace and with a deep connection to the Divine.

The only reality that I have is this one. The only feelings that I have are the ones that I feel, the ones that I am experiencing now. The only love that I feel is the eternal love for the Beloved.

In my quiet moments I think of you.
In my busy time, you are present in my mind.
When I dream… I dream of you.
You are so present in my mind and occupying the seat of honor in my heart.

Angel trumpets play your song like the sweet fragrance that lingers in the air at night, carried out with the notes of intoxicating moments of love that I share with my Beloved as we surrender into the arms of love.

I've come to realize how precious the small things in life are, the unspoken words the actions that mount up to be large and significant. Those smaller tasks are easier to carry out than the big ones. And then we can string them like a precious sting of pearls that can be offered to the Beloved.

I have fallen in love with life an unknown virus has unexpectedly entered my body, expanding to take over body, mind and spirit. I am dizzy intoxicated nothing looks the same. Vibrant colors enter my eyes and dance in my mind like melodies and sounds never heard before, the air touches my skin and I feel aroused like the first time I was passionately touched by my lover. If you want to take me this is the perfect time for me to go, but I have one request before I go send me back as soon as you can so I can experience the ecstasy of life that I am feeling right now.

*Like a mirror my soul displays the
secrets that I am reveling to you.
Vulnerable I become as I open up, Lord
you don't give me any other choice.
What can I do when the eyes of the
beloved stare at me? They melt me like
an ice cube melts in the warm sun.
I am a prisoner of my soul and a
co creator of my destiny, my soul is
talking to you.*

Walking down the forest a caterpillar fell down and landed in your heart slowly moving going round and round nested comfortably creating a cocoon in your heart.
Nurtured by love, kindness, affection and passion it turned into a pearlescent butterfly that flew to freedom right out of your heart.

Dreaming of a bed created by a million rose pedals where we roll around in the arms of love. The fantasy of two bodies mingled, woven as a carpet of fine linen and satin where there is no beginning and no end, being in the now open receptive wet and wild, mild and sensual. I come across your eyes and your smile. My heart skips a beat but it is fully alive and then the climax of emotions and feelings, who is who at this point, we are one.

Love thee like the ocean loves the beach and receives the gentle and passionate caress of the waters of life be open to the seductive qualities that the Beloved has to offer you. Love deeply and passionately, love the moment and love life, because you are worth it.

I am the essence of nature, I am the rain that comes to create moisture in your life, I am the sun that wraps around you and keeps you warm, I am like the ocean you can dive into me explore my depths, I am the moon that gives you the inspiration and guides you at night, I am the wind strong and kind. Just don't try to possess me because how can you possess a part of nature a part of the Divine.

I live my life because of you, I sing a new song to you today my inspiration and love flows because you move me, you stir my soul and create a turmoil of emotions. I feel because of you, I look for your playful eyes to rest in mine. Look at me my love, lover and seduce me, it doesn't take much. I look for you because I know you are there and the desire grows to be consumed by your love.

ERNESTO ORTIZ
Biography

Ernesto Ortiz was born in Mexico City, in 1951. As a child he frequently visited the family's coffee plantation, where he learned a life style that will later mark the path of his teachings, influenced by "curaciones" and other practices carried by the Shamans of this land. At the age of 14, he went as an exchange student to Michigan, returning later to his native country to finish High School. Around the age of 17, he started exploring mind expanding with teacher plants. He moved to San Diego, California where he studied textiles and photography, and at 21 his passion to study and photograph native cultures and "shamanism" brought him on a two-year trip to South America. Upon his return to California, he established a business importing textiles from Ecuador, Peru and Bolivia; worked as a photographer for Kali Productions -an LA based company; and opened a retail business dealing with crystals and accessories. In 1990, inner-calling and a desire to share with others the accumulation of experiences and the ability to develop mind work stirred Ernesto to a new direction. In 1988 he moved to Florida where he founded "Journey to the Heart", a company dedicated to the improvement of consciousness and the well-being of people. He has been featured in Allure, Cosmopolitan, and Selecta Magazines as one of the best massage therapists from coast to coast; in TV programs such as 'Despierta America" (the Spanish version of Good Morning America), "Primer Impacto", Galavision, Telemundo/NBC; in radio shows like "Asi contigo" and WLRN Public Radio, reaching an international audience of over 86 million people. Ernesto has two children and makes his home base in Miami, Fl.